T0278301

RAILWAY ENTHUSIASM IN TWENTY-FIRST-CENTURY BRITAIN

JOSEPH ROGERS

AMBERLEY

Front, top: Class 66 no. 66743 at Aviemore station on the Strathspey Railway, October 2021. (Author); *bottom*: GWR 7800 Class no. 7822 *Foxcote Manor* departs Bishops Lydeard on the West Somerset Railway during the 2022 Spring Steam Gala. (Author)

Back: The Moors Valley Railway near Ringwood, Hampshire. (Author)

First published 2024

Amberley Publishing
The Hill, Stroud,
Gloucestershire, GL5 4EP

www.amberley-books.com

ISBN: 978 1 3981 1668 9 (print)
ISBN: 978 1 3981 1669 6 (ebook)

British Library Cataloguing in Publication Data.
A catalogue record for this book is available from the British Library.

Typeset in 10pt on 13pt Celeste.
Typesetting by SJmagic DESIGN SERVICES, India.
Printed in the UK.

Contents

Introduction

The Origins of Railway Enthusiasts in Britain

The phenomenon that is railway enthusiasm, trainspotting or (as it is termed in the United States) 'railfanning', has been around almost as long as the railways themselves. Even as early as the nineteenth century, publications on both sides of the Atlantic regularly kept those with an eye for the progression of railway and railroad networks informed about the latest innovations in technology. Though there might initially have been more of an academic fanbase for the technical virtues of railways, the general public were no less interested, particularly as mass transportation developed to encompass the working class, commuters and those seeking opportunities away from their homes.

But as the twentieth century dawned, a new breed of interest also emerged that in Britain centred largely around the development of steam locomotives and their use on the large network of main and branch lines, operating in a variety of fashions across a number of different railway companies. Classes of locomotive built by different manufacturers and working different kinds of trains suited to each locality and their requirements across Britain became the interest of many on the sidelines, not necessarily working for the railways themselves. Observers would stand at the ends of platforms, on bridges, along embankments and on the threshold of railway yards, capturing, noting and describing both the regular and irregular forms that trains could be seen in across the nation.

As wartime came and went, a huge shift away from steam began to change the face of Britain's railways forever. Sleek, loud, thundering diesel locomotives and their electric counterparts took the baton of the railways' workload and with that emerged both a new breed of enthusiast and the beginning of divisions with the existing ones. Class types and, with the arrival of the TOPS system in the 1970s, a universal system for locomotive and rolling stock numbers became chapters and verses for the spotters and photographers that had now established themselves firmly on the railway scene, forming a hobby that would go on to branch off into many different areas and disciplines.

Decades on, the railways were producing children, grandchildren and great-grandchildren with lasting legacies to fulfil in railway enthusiasm. But the railways were also in decline, giving way to the motor car and eventually being chopped, changed and reduced into the

Railway and Locomotive Engineering was an American publication in the early twentieth century that covered 'railway motive power, rolling stock, and appliance' of the time. It often featured railway innovations from elsewhere in the world, including Britain. Pictured in a 1903 issue is a London & South Western Railway steam railcar. (Author's collection)

Even by the time of the turn of the previous century, the variety of steam locomotives on the British network and of railway companies saw onlookers take note of classes and numbers. Pictured is LNWR Dreadnought Class No. 1395 *Archimedes* at London's Euston station *c.* 1890. (Library of Congress, Prints & Photographs Division, LC-B2-2247-8)

People often refer to the 'Golden Age of Steam' as being the peak of railway prowess in Britain, but younger enthusiasts might argue otherwise. This photograph, dated 1934, shows the stationmaster at Edinburgh Waverley awaiting the departure of LNER A4 Class No. 4482 *Golden Eagle*. (Public domain, with thanks to Nationaal Archief)

1960s and 1970s. By this time, enthusiasts had begun to look fondly back on the steam age, with some rejecting the reality of modern technology altogether. The preservation movement got underway and hobbies like modelling allowed people to continue to live in a past associated with their golden age. Some held onto this for their relatives' sake as the progressing to diesel and electric saw changes in the workforce and irked many whose fathers, mothers and grandparents had worked so hard during a period for Britain's railways that was becoming increasingly romanticised.

As the preservation movement was beginning for the steam-era fans, platform spotters and photographers were awaiting the arrival of high-speed trains, tilting trains, a plethora of multiple units, test trains as well as the occasional glory run for what remained of Britain's steam engines.

The evolution of the enthusiast continued. By the 1990s, preserved railways were themselves becoming the spark to light the flame of the late twentieth and early twenty-first-century rail enthusiasts and saw the diesel era itself become part of that heritage movement. Multiple units and the standardisation of many services again saw older generations clamber for rare and occasional locomotive-hauled movements on the main line while the next generation began noting the increasing variety of DMUs and EMUs throughout the nation. As the year 2000 came and went, the internet began to change what the typical rail enthusiast could achieve and gave birth to a true cohort of twenty-first-century rail enthusiasts. As one generation held onto the past, another was there eager to continue the passion for the future.

A Brief Note on Today's Charms and Challenges

This title aims to explore how these enthusiasts have grown to keep the phenomenon alive, the disciplines of this hobby that exist in the modern age, and the challenges that its followers may face. Though these disciplines may at times be wildly different from those of past generations, the overall concept has changed very little and with tools at their disposal that those 100 years ago would never have dreamed of, the potential to extract more enjoyment from the hobby has been higher than ever before. But being an enthusiast of anything today is not without challenges or controversy in a world much more delicate and reactive than before the turn of the millennium.

Mentioned in brief will be a number of topics that are incredibly sensitive in twenty-first-century Britain and, indeed, the world. These range from political issues around the railways themselves, the economy, the validity of public transport and the environment, as well as broad societal conversation points around misogyny, discrimination, racism, ageism, pureism, traditionalism, ableism and shifts in cultural change that are unique to the times that we live in. While feeling strongly that these issues need to be talked about within the context of the railway hobby (something tackled in a variety of ways currently, both positively and negatively), the author is by no means an expert on the deep-rooted details of some of these important issues. Many others consider themselves to be and a small number are. But the author does hope that raising them here might prompt further discussion about how they might be managed and how attitudes might be improved around them.

1

Children of the 1990s: The First Twenty-First-Century Rail Enthusiasts

Though it is easy to think that the first twenty-first-century rail enthusiasts came after the year 2000, it could be argued that those born in the late 1980s and 1990s were the first to mature enough to a point of genuine and meaningful interest in railways as the next century dawned. Though, like their parents and grandparents, an interest may have been formed by seeing main-line operations in and around their home towns and cities, for many children of the 1990s, it was the well-established preservation movement that began what, for some, would become a lifelong love affair.

But railway ancestry can also play a part. With the railways forming such a large part of Britain's workforce, tales of relatives once working the rails would be equally important in bringing an interest to a younger audience. Weekends away with grandparents to relive the old days of steam would be common for many a child, regardless of wealth or background and adding to an interest in the wider railway hobby.

Indeed, both of these aspects were the case for the author during this decade. Though the author didn't know it at the time, great-grandfather Richard 'Harry' Williams rose through the ranks from cleaner, to fireman, to driver of steam locomotives during the first half of the twentieth century. His career followed the evolution of Britain's railway companies in the Shrewsbury (and later Walsall) areas, first cleaning for the LNWR, then firing and driving for the LMS and eventually British Rail before succumbing to stomach cancer in 1960. His granddaughter (the author's mother) was never an enthusiast herself, but on annual holidays from the West Midlands to North Wales she would use heritage railways and railway museums to provide ample entertainment for the family. In turn this formed an interest in her children for any kind of train, whether it be the narrow-gauge steam at the Talyllyn Railway (considered to be the first of the preserved railways) or a grubby Centro Sprinter at Walsall station. There was never an expectation to pursue a career in railways, but carrying a baton of enthusiasm was always going to be a result of this early exposure to them. The same can be said for countless others that were lucky enough to grow up with such memories.

Richard Henry 'Harry' Williams was born on
4 February 1903 in Coleham, Shrewsbury. His railway
career may have begun as a teenage carriage cleaner
at Shrewsbury station before joining the ranks as
a locomotive cleaner, fireman and later driver for
LNWR, LMS and British Rail. His granddaughter
Karen anecdotally remembers tales relayed of his
workings up to Holyhead and moving of freight
around Bescot during the Second World War. At
one point he worked out of Ryecroft Shed. He died
of stomach cancer in 1960 at the age of fifty-seven.
Pictured are himself (left) and his wife Kathleen
(right). (Author's collection)

For others, visiting heritage lines may have been accompanied by an introduction to modelling. By this time, the railway modelling industry was certainly matured and a perfect way for friends and family from the older generations to teach and interact with their children and grandchildren who might otherwise have been on the cusp of being flung into the digital age of entertainment. Whether distracted or not in later life, the residual railway information taught at an early age would remain for many, only to be extracted and made use of as they themselves became adults into the twenty-first century.

Of course, children's entertainment did ultimately have a say too. *Thomas the Tank Engine & Friends* still saw airtime on television alongside *Teletubbies*, *Postman Pat* and *Fireman Sam*, and the books became entry points for young readers picking from the bookshelf, lending from a library or being gifted hand-me-downs from those for which trains may not have been so inspiring. For some, this was the route that encouraged parents to take them to heritage railways or modelling exhibitions – to realise that there is a reality to the fiction. In truth, the 'Thomas fandom' has continued to produce its own arm of enthusiasm, linked more to the pop culture scene and divorced in many ways from the railways themselves, but in essence it is no less connected to them by association.

The 1990s also marked the final days of anything resembling the nationalised entity that was British Rail. Though this may not have been forefront in the minds of the children

Above and below: While there are no known railway workers on the author's paternal side, the Rogers family in Wednesbury were prolific metal workers. Both Joseph Rogers (1866–1949) and his son Joseph Rogers (1887–1960) worked as drillers on bridge girders for local firm Patent Shaft. A rare surviving example of Patent Shaft's bridge output remains (at the time of writing) at Toller Porcorum, Dorset and once carried the Bridport Railway. It was at one stage earmarked for removal by National Highways. (Author)

An early encounter that the author had with a heritage railway in 1994 at the Teifi Valley Railway in South Wales. The locomotive is Simplex Motor Rail 4wDM No. 11111 *Sammy*, built in 1951. Memories formed from these holidays would later mature beyond the turn of the century into a fully formed enthusiasm for railways. (Author's collection)

The author cannot remember having ever gone to the Lakeside & Haverthwaite Railway, but this photograph suggests otherwise featuring the family in front of Austerity 0-6-0ST locomotive *Cumbria*. The locomotive has since run on other heritage lines. (Author's collection)

For West Midlands families, North Wales has long been a popular tourist destination, in part thanks to its heritage and narrow-gauge railways. The Ffestiniog Railway (Rheilffordd Ffestiniog) is one of the best. This photo, taken of the author (right) and his brother (left) in the year 2000, appears to show Double Fairlie locomotive *David Lloyd George* at Blaenau Ffestiniog. The image was donated to the railway as part of the 100 Photos campaign during the Covid-19 pandemic. (Author's collection)

Above and below: Loco haulage was still a common occurrence on passenger services during the early 1990s. Class 50s roamed the West of England Main Line between Exeter and London Waterloo. Pictured are Nos 50002 and 50050 at Exeter Central in June 1990. Exeter St Davids sees a Class 47/4 arriving with a set of air-con Mk 2 coaches in July 1991. (Richard Szwejkowski)

Multiple units spread in use and variety as the twentieth century came to a close. Units like that pictured, a Class 150 *Sprinter* in Regional Railways livery, ferried the author as a child from Walsall to relatives and beyond. This unit, No. 150128, is seen at Crewe in August 1996. (Dave Hitchborne, CC BY-SA 2.0)

Left: Despite them being introduced in the late 1950s, the author remembers being seated behind the driver in Class 101 DMUs on rural Welsh branch lines in the 1990s. Pictured is No. 101679 at Marple in 1997. (Public domain)

Below: A similar view can be found behind the driver of a Class 115 on the West Somerset Railway. (Author)

of this decade, their awareness of the colourful brands and TOCs gracing the early 2000s would have stemmed from the shift to privatisation and the political nature of the railway industry under both John Major and Tony Blair. In later decades, the more astute twenty-first-century rail enthusiasts may have come to appreciate this in retrospect or learn that their knowledge of this time in railway history was linked intimately to the political history of their nation.

Ultimately, those turning into teenagers or, regardless of age, becoming a more mature enthusiast during the mid-2000s would become the first group of independent twenty-first-century rail enthusiasts, taking the joy they had earned or learned from their '90s ventures and applying it in their first solo experiences of train travel, modelling, spotting or volunteering within Britain's growing railway hobby.

The Talyllyn Railway in Wales became the first railway in the world to be preserved by volunteers in 1951. Though it may irk some enthusiasts, younger fans of the railway often enjoy the 'Thomas-esque' face placed at the front of No. 3 *Sir Handel*, as seen in 2008. (Public domain)

2

Heritage Railways and Railway Tourism

As touched on earlier, heritage railways have, for many twenty-first-century enthusiasts, been the catalyst for growing a tangible passion for railways. For those who were never old enough to see the romance and drama of main-line steam, the availability of nostalgic steam railways, however long or short, remains a real thrill for youngsters, adequate joy for families generally and a natural habitat for older generations of enthusiasts to relive, remember and continue their love of the past.

But their development has been accelerated through the turn of the century from eccentric origins to professional businesses in order to survive in the competitive and regulated modern-day tourism industry. In most cases, heritage railways began as an output of the rail enthusiasts themselves, banding together to save engines from scrap, buy up rolling stock and reopening old branch lines during a time of great change for Britain's railways in 1960s and 1970s.

Stories told in other publications, like *Tales of the WSR*, and those covering the first preserved railways like the Talyllyn Railway, as well as information concerning individuals like David Shepherd and Alan Pegler, describe the passion of those keen to selflessly keep history alive for future generations, or in some cases simply to continue their own personal endeavours. Others instead document the rebellious nature of setting up a preservation movement, creating a fun and carefree outlet for enjoying a railway without being stifled by the need to be efficient, punctual or even in most cases safe or profitable.

Many of those that were around at this time, regardless of whether they were involved or not, would argue that these tinpot origins of the majority of Britain's heritage railways should remain at their core, but the reality is that as time has gone by and these efforts have themselves become an important cottage industry, the need to smarten up and run professionally has become necessary for these operations to survive in the twenty-first century.

Today, whether those working on them like it or not, heritage railways are an important part of the tourism industry and can often contribute not only to the hobby, but to local businesses, communities and economies. While they still hold onto key concepts like volunteering, owning groups, galas, trusts and shareholders that each support the venture

The East Somerset Railway, based at Cranmore in the Mendips, was opened as a heritage railway in the early 1970s by artist David Shepherd (1931–2017) as a place to run his privately owned locomotives: Class 9F No. 92203 *Black Prince* and Standard 4 No. 75029 *The Green Knight*. Today the railway continues to run for the public. Pictured is Andrew Barclay Works locomotive *Lady Nan*, which is also privately owned by a railway volunteer. (Author)

Steam locomotives are still the biggest draw for tourists and families visiting heritage lines today. Their costly upkeep has seen some operations look to diversify with alternative traction, whereas others double down as 'steam railways' relying largely on their appeal for business. GWR Large Prairie No. 5199 is pictured at Bishops Lydeard on the West Somerset Railway, having moved from the Llangollen Railway during its closure because of the Covid-19 pandemic. (Author)

Left: Experiencing the footplate. The author pictured during a light engine move in the cab of No. 5199. Such moments remain ingrained in the memories of those lucky enough to get such opportunities. (Author)

Below: LNER Class A3 No. 4472 *Flying Scotsman*, built in 1923 and owned by the National Railway Museum, remains the poster child for the heritage railway movement in the eyes of the wider public. Here it is pictured in preparation for its centenary year at King's Cross station, London. (Author)

SR West Country Class No. 21C127 *Taw Valley* at the Severn Valley Railway showing its temporary livery and name, *Elizabeth II*, from 2022. Despite being widely publicised as temporary to celebrate Elizabeth II's platinum jubilee, a small but vocal enthusiast following protested. They were largely ignored and the stunt proved very popular with the wider public and enthusiasts themselves. (Alan Land)

Somerset & Dorset Joint Railway 7F No. 53808 gets turned at Minehead station in 2018. This popular and reliable locomotive was at the West Somerset Railway for many years before politics saw its owners move it elsewhere. Events like this occur frequently behind the scenes in such environments. (Author)

in their own way, there is also now the need for due diligence, compliance and sound business planning, backed by paid staff, government funding, charity work, marketing campaigns and a well-established social media presence.

The refusal to accept this by a larger-than-needed number of enthusiasts is startling and the 'old guard' spouting such naivety can have a negative impact on youth. Upon visiting a well-known heritage line in the Midlands, the author overheard a uniformed volunteer proclaim that the forthcoming Santa services were turning it into 'another ****ing

Disneyland' and that railway galas were the only way to bring people onto a railway. This contradiction among heritage rail personnel is a common one, with many failing to recognise that the profits and positive public perception earned (especially by younger enthusiasts and their families) from Christmas services would in turn ensure that enough money, footfall and support was available to justify the following year's steam gala and the high costs of transporting visiting locomotives to the event. It is only in recent years that more streetwise, adaptable heritage lines have begun to stray from the traditional gala event, electing to make them relevant to wider audiences with main-line visitors, support from TOCs as potential recruitment opportunities and tie-ins to other trends like national celebrations, sporting events and pop culture. It cannot be underestimated just how important events themed

Despite the need to move to events with wider appeal, enthusiasts still flock to special running days and railway galas, as evidenced by this scene at the Llangollen Railway's Steel, Steam & Stars event from a decade ago. (Author's collection)

Where main line and heritage railways collide. The Swanage Railway in Dorset not only acts as a heritage operation, but facilitates trains from the main line and acts as a Park & Ride for tourists courtesy of its stations at Norden and Swanage. Pictured leaving Swanage in 2022 is SR Battle of Britain Class No. 34072 *257 Squadron*. (Author)

The preservation movement continues to break boundaries in certain areas, such as when A1 Class No. 60163 *Tornado* was built in 2008. This was the first British steam locomotive to be built in Britain since 1960. Other efforts are under way to recreate other bygone classes of steam locomotive. (Colour-enhanced public domain image)

around wizards, *The Polar Express*, illuminations and even dinosaurs have become in the context of keeping heritage railways financially viable and for those reluctant to run catering services, entities like Fox & Edwards Events have arisen to do the work for them.

The Severn Valley Railway's temporary re-liverying of SR West Country Class 21C127 *Taw Valley* in 2022 brought the opposing views of purists and hobbyists to light when a small but vocal minority protested against the choice of colour – bright purple. This publicity stunt, done so for Elizabeth II's platinum jubilee, was a smart and joyous initiative by the railway giving them a platform to draw in interest not only from railfans young and old, but also the wider British public and even those from abroad focussing their attention on anything and everything related to the celebration of the royal family. In turn, coverage in railway magazines, newspapers, blogs and even TV and radio would have massively benefitted the SVR and the running events around that time, not to mention the ever important social media coverage. Yet the small number of pedantic protesters were adamant that it tarnished the reputation of the railway, the purity of *Taw Valley* and the integrity of their precious hobby. Some would happily have foregone the additional support, publicity and funds, to keep the locomotive green.

Attitudes like this stem often from a lack of understanding of why heritage railways exist today and how they are required to run themselves. They should serve primarily as education venues, to teach younger generations about the vital importance of Britain's railways while also offering something for older generations to enjoy. Volunteers and visitors alike will forever be at odds with those working tirelessly to keep them going when faced with issues like this, especially when some heritage lines themselves shy away from their challenges as twenty-first-century operations. The lack of transparency comes to light in some interesting ways. Visitors to one heritage line in 2019 approached the author to enquire why 'Delay Repay' wasn't accommodated following the failure of a steam locomotive hauling a service train. Being told that the line was a) privately run, b) not part of national network and c) charity funded came as a shock to them, as did the concept that providing a cash refund would actually increase the chance of such failures happening again, by taking funds directly from the piggybank that helped keep the locomotives in running condition. Had the railway in question been more open in communicating to the public they were a charity-led educational heritage project, rather than pretending to be an extension of the main-line railway network stuck in the past, then the attitude to the locomotive failure may have been viewed in an entirely different light.

But the ease of access to heritage railways as tourist attractions for a wide audience also forms an important starting point for new enthusiasts as well as an opening for contemporary enthusiasts by allowing them to explore the arms of spotting, photography and history in a largely safe and accessible manner. The proliferation of photographs and feedback on the internet and social media today forms crucial publicity material for the attractions themselves and creates a largely positive dialogue between railway and enthusiast that is rarely seen with main-line operators and certainly didn't exist as intimately as it did in the previous century.

As with anything social media related, there is of course a dark side and the ability for detractors to openly slate and destroy the hard work of their colleagues and fellow hobbyists. This open interaction with organisations of any size can often be abused and naysayers regularly make their points known with little maturity or reasonableness.

As time has moved on, some of the key innovations in diesel traction have been celebrated in the heritage movement, warranting their own strong following. The Class 55 'Deltics' have become star attractions at heritage railway diesel galas, such as the 2018 event on the West Somerset Railway. Pictured is No. 55019 *Royal Highland Fusilier* on the turntable at Minehead station. (Author)

Right: Class 50s also have a significant following, with spotters of their day often lamenting occasions when they were substituted by 'Duffs' (Class 47s). Many are still running in preservation. Pictured is a Class 50 at Bewdley station in 2022, thought to be No. 50035 *Ark Royal*. (Author)

Below: Once seen as the modern successors to the steam era, many diesel locomotives have themselves become historic, with many scrapped and withdrawn and others faithfully preserved. Not all can be saved, however. Class 33 No. 33046 (or D6564) was finally disposed of in April 2023, with only a cab end remaining in the hands of a private collector. Pictured at the East Lancashire Railway's Buckley Wells Depot in 2022. (Author – taken from the yard with permission from the East Lancashire Railway)

Many Class 33s are preserved, with some cleared for main line running. Two are based at Williton and owned by the Diesel and Electric Preservation Group (DEPG). D6566 is seen about to depart Bishops Lydeard in 2019. (Author)

Appearances of guest steam locomotives, and the costs associated with moving and running them, make steam galas prohibitive in times of financial pressure. The appeal to the wider public is small when compared to festive and seasonal events, or those tapping into children's characters and pop culture. Pictured is Caledonian Railway Class 439 No. 419 a long way from home at Williton on the West Somerset Railway. (Author)

Equally, the different generations of enthusiast within an organisation can form destructive environments for the heritage movement. The steam/diesel divide is perhaps most noticeable within the heritage railway setting and is still majority led by the ideals of the past. Others recognise a diversity in operations as a wholly beneficial aspect that allows a number of different audiences to be pleased at once, along with the obvious benefits of adaptability and improvisation by having a variety of rolling stock to utilise. It is no surprise that the heritage railways with more open attitudes on how they run their operations often correlate with those that are more financially secure and generously supported by volunteers and visitors.

The result is that the best of Britain's heritage railways very much embrace those whom they have inspired into the twenty-first century. The age of digital communications, online or contactless ticket systems, interactive social media and gimmicky trends such as memes are ways for them to continue the inspiration of countless youngsters without isolating the very people that began the heritage movement in the first place. Survival of these organisations, especially in recent years defined by the pandemic, politics and climate change, has largely been down to the success of modern publicity, support from a wider demographic and an openness from within to change. But key to this is that enthusiasm from old and young, without which there will be no heritage railways in the future.

Seeds continue to be sewn in the preservation movement even today. Increasingly, younger bands of enthusiasts are saving multiple units that, while being twentieth century in origin, have ended their lives a decade or two into the twenty-first century.

Unfortunately, efforts to preserve both diesel and electric multiple units (DMUs and EMUs) come up against many hurdles that the previous locomotive preservation movements did not. Aside from the costs of acquiring more complex, technologically advanced units

More recently withdrawn locomotives are still thankfully being preserved. Class 37 No. 37308 was the last Class 37 to be built in 1965 and was withdrawn in 2007. It is, at the time of writing, being worked on at the Severn Valley Railway, but was previously at Lydney, where it is pictured in 2019. (Author)

Above and left: The cycle of restoration and re-restoration can see an enthusiast follow the rebirth of some locomotives several times over. Pictured in 2018 is Class 52 D1010 *Western Campaigner* prior to a gearbox failure and later under restoration at Williton in 2022. By the time of publication, this locomotive may well be running again. (Author)

Below: Railway galas have themselves come under threat in recent times, with the need for heritage lines to host profit-making events. In the past, they were often guided by enthusiasm and not cashflow. Events at the Severn Valley Railway in recent years have seen good turnouts, aided by unusual guests from both heritage and main-line railways. Pictured is GBRf Class 69 No. 69005 *Eastleigh* at Kidderminster, converted in the early 2020s from Class 56 No. 56007. (Author)

Right and below: The Pacer classes of DMU, despite being both hated and joked about by enthusiasts when introduced in the 1980s, have since sprouted a light-hearted but considerable following among younger enthusiasts, akin to that of the Lada or Trabant in the motoring world. Many have since been withdrawn and reside as cheap runarounds on heritage railways. Pictured is Class 143 No. 143618 in main-line service between Dawlish and Starcross in 2017 and two Pacer class DMUs awaiting their second life at the Telford Steam Railway in 2023. (Author)

Though restricted by speed limits and coaching stock, seeing 'old friends' is a big part of visiting heritage railways for enthusiasts. Pictured is Class 50 No. 50050 (numbered D400) at Yeovil Railway Centre in 2013, which appeared in a photograph earlier in this book. (Author)

being higher than those of previous trains and that technology requiring its own levels of knowledge and maintenance, the simple fact of moving a multiple unit poses challenges different to that of locomotives. As units with multiple 'cars', road transport costs are prohibitive, storage difficult and hauling only an option for areas connected to the main line.

In the case of EMUs, no heritage lines exist that can reasonably accommodate third rail or overhead power (the Epping Ongar Railway perhaps a notable exception), reducing most preservation efforts to static displays, holiday home conversions, museums or cafés. More ambitious groups might seek to have the stock hauled with a locomotive.

Though DMU preservation has seen notable success, from main-line running DEMUs, to preserved Pacers convening for galas, the EMU scene has been limited in scope, resulting in even some of the most noted examples being lost. Only one car remains as a preservation effort from a unit class that holds onto the record for the world's fastest third-rail electric – the Class 442 'Plastic Pig'. Other notable EMU preservation efforts include a Class 309/ AM9 once used as a departmental test train and an entire four-car Class 315 set destined for the Llanelli & Mynydd Mawr Railway, which required movement by rail and road. Both of these projects have been supported by a considerable number of incredibly ambitious teenage enthusiasts often combining a forceful will to save the units with a healthy dose of youthful naivety – perhaps not all too different from those climbing on Jubilees and Halls at Barry Scrapyard all those decades ago.

What is key is that no matter what the remit, scope, era or theme of any heritage railway, that they recognise their place in bringing new people to the hobby, in addition to holding onto the knowledge, passion and dedication of those already in it.

Above and overleaf: Shunting locomotives often have local histories that heritage lines can help preserve.

North British shunter No. 27414 worked at GKN Sankey in Hadley near Telford and is now preserved at the Telford Steam Railway.

The Barclay industrial shunter known as 'the ROF' seen at the West Somerset Railway, used to work at the Royal Ordinance Factory in Puriton near Bridgwater.

Class 08 No. 08164 *Prudence* at the East Lancashire Railway is one of many such locomotives preserved. Others still work the main-line shunting yards and depots, while others look to the future with hydrogen and electric power. (Author – taken from the yard with permission from the East Lancashire Railway)

Electric Multiple Unit AM9 / Class 309 No. 309624 ran services up to London, Colchester and Clacton-on-Sea during the 1960s and 1970s. Later in life it served as a departmental Class 960 testing in-cab signalling equipment before being saved, with the aim of preservation, by an ambitious and young group of enthusiasts. Pictured at the Lavendar Line in 2022, its fate remains uncertain at the time of writing. (Author – taken from the track bed with permission from the CEPG)

3

Railway Modelling

Railway modelling, or model railroading as it is known in the United States, is an arm of the railway hobby with origins that date back well into the 1800s as crude, whimsical facsimiles of what was being run on the real rails. Today, like tourism and heritage railways, it is a multi-million-pound industry supported by large companies and organisations with stakes both within the UK and beyond.

The growth of a railway enthusiast and the ebbing and flowing of the passion around the rest of life's activities develops largely in two phases. While these phases can be applied to almost any area of railway enthusiasm, the time, money and dedication often required to fully make the most of railway modelling means that these phases are perhaps accentuated.

This photograph, doctored to feature steam rising from the chimney, shows an N-gauge model of GWR Hall Class No. 4951 *Pendeford Hall*. Modelling allows for bygone scenes to be recreated – this locomotive was withdrawn in 1964 and scrapped. (Author's collection)

The G-Scale Model Railway Garden at the Chicago Botanic Garden in Cook County, Illinois, hosts an impressive control room where rolling stock can be seen on display. American model railroading has a keen following in the UK. (Author)

Phase one begins at childhood level, where the endless running round of model locomotives, through tunnels, across points and crossing other trains as they go, is arguably more engaging and inspiring than the real thing. There's an intimacy that children can appreciate in a model railway, getting up close and personal with tiny trains and models, not so easily done on a full-sized railway. Equally, model railways are tangible. Trains can be picked up and put down, points can be switched, carriages can be uncoupled and this level of interactivity can become an absorbing and engaging way for kids to get really passionate and fixated on trains. During those formative years, model railways can become the sole outlet for railway enthusiasm in youngsters, right through until later teenage years, by which time many have learned the practical skills to build and maintain their own, even if financed or supported from family, friends or a local club. More often than not, all of this begins with an introduction to an existing layout, owned and built by a relative, or shown at a local exhibition. Genesis layouts might be that of something like Brio, before moving onto the more technical and delicate model railway formats using different gauges of track.

Then comes the hiatus. As teenage years come and go, other factors in life such as finances, employment, relationships and indulgences, as well as the constant day-to-day goings on, see the interest in modelling tail off. That new locomotive gives way to the car's MOT test, the hour testing whether the signalling works gets eaten up by after-work drinks or the late shift and, eventually, the layout has to move altogether to make way for the baby's crib. Though these factors have always been at odds with modelling, they are perhaps more pronounced now than ever, with the hobby itself costing considerable sums and a plethora of extra-curricular activities competing to make use of our precious time and

The American influence in Britain is seen here at this outdoor model railway fronting the streetside in Kentisbeare, Devon. (Author)

Before the rise of electric train sets, tinplate wind-up toys, such as this made by Bing Germany for the UK market circa 1920s, were a way for young and old to enjoy railways in the living room. (Author's collection)

money. Parenthood, drinking, partying, sport, the outdoors and, more recently, video games offer generally more sociable, cheaper pastimes, which push modelling (and often other areas of the railway hobby) to the backburner during these all-important years of adult life.

It is beyond this where phase two begins. Those who are lucky enough to find a rhythm to life, particularly as the kids leave for university, the job becomes more rewarding and the social life calms down, are able to come back to railway modelling, armed with more disposable income, better timekeeping and a renewed passion and drive to carry on from where their childhood left off. It is at this point when parents might complete the cycle and introduce their children or other youngsters to their own 'phase one'.

The industry understands this. PECO, still manufacturing model railway track from the small village of Beer, in Devon, created the popular tourism venture 'Pecorama' back in 1975 with the aim of inspiring children through its model exhibition and ride-on railway (the latter being one of the longest 7¼-inch-gauge lines in the UK), in the hope that they might one day return with their own children and invest their money back into the company that ignited their childhood interest. And it works. Visitors in the twenty-first century are often formed of family units from up and down the country who first enjoyed the attraction and the Beer Heights Light Railway in the 1980s and 1990s, returning to offer their children the same enjoyment that they experienced thanks to their parents.

It is a concept that is repeated (not always intentionally) by heritage railways, museums, theme parks and other businesses in tourism, whereby generations work to pass on their enjoyment through memory and nostalgia. Repeat business forms over the course of two or more generations.

However, that is not to say that the companies like PECO don't try to make themselves relevant for a younger, twenty-first-century audience directly. Though the 'inspire them young, sell to them old' business model continues to be a longer-term plan for many such organisations, the likes of PECO, Hornby, KATO, Bachmann and Marklin, put a lot of effort into developing the latest technological advances in modelling to more directly grab a hold of twenty-first-century modellers. Layouts can now be controlled through smartphones, DCC offers varied lighting and audio options and the use of computing generally now sees large and sophisticated layouts make use of automatic signalling, platform announcements, day/night cycles and more.

This image, dated April 1951 and taken in Europe, shows the public's fascination with model railways from the last century. (Public domain, with thanks to Nationaal Archief)

Above: The vast variety of locomotives of liveries means companies have to select what might appeal to a broad enough audience. Network SouthEast has its own keen following, with Class 08 No. 08600 shown here on display at the PECO model shop in Devon. (Author)

Below: While Hornby might be a household name for the wider public, companies like PECO are just as notable to modellers. Unlike many British model brands, PECO still manufacture in the UK. Their headquarters are seen here in Beer, Devon, in 2019. (Public domain)

Left and below: Some model trains are never destined to run. Class 47 No. 47716 *Duke of Edinburgh's Award* was gifted to a non-enthusiast as a personal display item and GWR Large Prairie No. 5109 represents the author's memorable footplate ride shown earlier in the book. Many collectors keep such models boxed and amass thousands of pounds worth of stock. (Author)

And new names are joining the hobby all the time. Revolution Trains, set up in 2014 by Mike Hale and former BBC news correspondent Ben Ando, work on the basis of making small production run items based on expression of interest, with a focus on contemporary rolling stock in N gauge. The recent resurgence of Absolute Aspects in 2022, who make bespoke signalling for most gauges out of a small workshop in Axminster, use 3D printing and social media among other modern innovations to produce made-to-order batches of fully functioning signals, including ground position lights, route indicator panels and signal gantries.

Cameras, photography and filming have also added immeasurably to the appeal of railway modelling post-2000, with GoPro and YouTube in particular bringing living, breathing model railways to a vast audience. 'Driver's Eye' videos using minute cameras on the front of a model train can take viewers through a layout created in incredible detail and even the older forms of media like modelling magazines depict layouts through photography that can make the most professional of layouts seem almost real.

Social media has also accelerated the interest in model railways among the masses, even if only for the time it takes to 'like' an Instagram or TikTok post. Videos depicting cats sitting on, playing with or ruthlessly attacking model railways garner millions of views and likes, as do seemingly endless garden railways and bars and restaurants that feature model trains as an attraction or gimmick. A wider audience is also drawn in by recognisable intellectual property and familiar faces. Hornby's Harry Potter range, led by the Hogwarts Express, draws on the popularity of a book series that has sold over 500 million copies worldwide and its series of record-breaking movies. Jools Holland, Sir Rod Stewart and Pete Waterman, all known beyond the railway hobby for their music endeavours, have featured in print, on television and on social media talking about their love for the hobby to a wider audience, as has James May of *Top Gear* fame. Both Hornby and PECO have had their staff become minor celebrities themselves: Montana Hoeren and Simon Kohler in Yesterday's *Hornby: A Model World* and *Railway Modeller* magazine's Steve Flint in Channel 5's *The Great Model Railway Challenge.*

The mainstream media have picked on some record-breaking model railways themselves that excite the broadest of international audiences. Heaton Lodge Junction, which reportedly cost upwards of £250,000 and was built in secret by Simon George, made the headlines in 2021 and has been admired at a number of venues by the general public. Miniatur Wunderland, in Hamburg, Germany, which is a major tourist attraction with a large social media following, continuously features on international TV with its constantly changing and expanding range of dioramas that showcase the extreme details that modellers can include when recreating entire towns and cities within a model railway.

In many ways it is easy to think that the twenty-first century is a comfortable time for Britain's railway modelling hobby, particularly when something like Covid-19 forced a lot of people indoors and back into more traditional pastimes. But it should not be underestimated how hard those involved work to compete with the endless barrage of new and trendy pastimes hitting the inboxes of enthusiasts young and old. What's important to note, however, is that the industry does manage to keep up, perhaps differentiating their approach as an industry to that of some heritage railways and other less business-like areas of the wider railway hobby. It is not as dead a hobby as many might believe and serves young enthusiasts in this century as well as it did in the last one.

Above: Setting the scene. A Class 08, No. 08513 made by Hornby, runs by a wintry level crossing as part of this layout. (Author's collection)

Below: Modern image layouts are very popular and require the latest liveries and branding. Pictured here is a Hornby-made Class 67 with a contemporary car and coffee chain shown in the surroundings. (Public domain image by Peter Glyn)

Above left: Absolute Aspects was established in 2011, from the original Roger Murray Colour Light Signals company. Today it makes bespoke model colour light signals and gantries in a variety of scales and sizes and is based out of Devon. (Absolute Aspects)

Above right: A model Class 55 Deltic D9006 *The Fife & Forfar Yeomanry*, made by Lima, sits on a demo layout complete with lineside workers and buildings. (Absolute Aspects)

4

Commuting, Transport and Travel

During the time between those two phases of railway modelling interest, trains can instead occupy a more practical place in most people's lives, particularly for those living in urban areas and using them to commute or travel on a regular basis. In lives completely defined by work, family and pleasure beyond railways, travel by train can often be the only outlet for what might otherwise be a passion left to waste until later life. Small, tokenistic gestures to the hobby can be made during a family holiday, driving past a heritage line without necessarily stopping to enjoy it, or on a city break with friends, where one might 'just pop to use the toilet' in that grand European terminus with all manner of strange and wonderful locomotives and units in platform.

The commute can also be the one time where a hectic life can allow a brief, perhaps pressured, time to appreciate the railways. Though diversions, cancellations and changes in rolling stock can anger the uninitiated and excite the pure enthusiast, those confined to the trappings of routine might find solace in travelling with a different multiple unit or an interest in a change in stopping pattern, just before that big, important 9 a.m. meeting.

Even for enthusiasts without those limitations like the retired, the young and the unemployed, travelling by train and using the railways is a pure and dedicated outlet for their interest. This is particularly relevant for 'bashers' – those who wish to travel behind certain classes of locomotive or unit, or even individual locomotives and units within a class. When this is combined with a journey that needs to be made, or during a holiday in an area with wholly unfamiliar rolling stock, the combination of joys and pastimes can be incredibly satisfying.

Other endeavours require more concentration and planning. These can vary from covering certain parts of the railway network (as per those in the Branch Line Society, for example) to alighting and boarding at certain stations. The latter is a trend that's increased in recent years following the popular YouTube series by Geoff Marshall, where he took to the rails so that he could visit every station in the UK, then continuing to visit new stations in subsequent videos. Many have since done the same, ticking off the latest stations as they open or revisiting those that have changed in some way.

There's also appeal in taking advantage of rare and unusual services, such as the Class 90-hauled London to Manchester trains that ran in 2022 in light of troubles

Above and below: For the author time off from work without a driving licence saw plenty of Class 159 action along the West of England Main Line, exploring on foot the Somerset, Dorset and Wiltshire borderlands. Today, the Class 159 (and closely related 158) provides a mild sense of nostalgia for these times, despite still being widely used on the network.

These photos show the author on board an unidentified Class 159 at Axminster in 2011, with No. 159011 in the opposing platform and No. 159002 at Gillingham, Dorset, heading to London Waterloo in 2014. (Author's collection/author)

Business travellers working in Kent and London might find themselves expensing journeys on Britain's fastest domestic train – the Class 395 run by Southeastern along HS1. Enthusiasts from elsewhere often make an effort to travel the 140-mph line. (Author)

Similarly, the practical PPM (Parry People Mover) provides thoughtless transport for many living and working in Stourbridge. But as a Class 139, they are something to behold for enthusiasts seeking unique operations across the country. Pictured is unit No. 139001 on a low loader at Tyseley in 2008 and again at Stourbridge Junction in 2019. (Author's collection/author)

experienced with Avanti West Coast services, or the three coupled GWR Class 150s that trundled their way from Exeter to Reading the same year in place of a regular IET train.

Such challenges and excursions on regular, timetabled services are often self-serving, giving satisfaction to the enthusiast alone or within a group and this gratification can justify the hobby for many. It's also a way for enthusiasts to be close to the industry and appreciate the wider challenges that railways take on. Those making use of service trains to enjoy their hobby frequently see the raw reality of Britain's railways, along with regular passengers and the staff that keep the trains rolling. In the twenty-first century, this can highlight both the good and bad, from the kind-hearted train manager making someone's day, to the racist bigot shoving themselves through first class. Strikes, delays and overcrowding aren't necessarily at the forefront of modellers' and spotters' minds, but are experienced wholeheartedly by the enthusiasts that use the railways regularly.

More widely, travel brings a more casual audience onto the railways. TV programmes hosted by the likes of Michael Portillo, Chris Tarrant and Tony Robinson inspire a broad viewership to travel by train both in the UK and abroad. Names like the Orient Express, Tokyo's 'Bullet Train' and even Amtrak's long-distance railway journeys have become household names here in Britain. Though such 'celebrity' services here are limited to steam rail tours – or lines like the Ffestiniog or North York Moors railways and the Caledonian

Simply waiting for a train can yield interesting results for the enthusiast. An MPV (Multiple-purpose Vehicle) DR98971 runs through Chatham in 2022. (Author)

Above and below: Enthusiasts born in the 1990s may well have an attachment to rolling stock introduced around the same time as themselves. Class 465 EMUs remain popular among Southeastern fans, whereas Thames Valley and Westcountry residents may prefer the Class 165 and 166 DMUs. (Author)

A refreshing change for commuters, but the end of an era for enthusiasts. Tears were shed during the Class 313's farewell tour in 2023. Pictured are No. 313205 and Class 377 No. 377474 at Barnham in 2022. (Public domain image by Alex Noble)

Right: What might seem mundane to some is of interest to others. A short trip to Liss from Peterfield sees the author travel on a Class 450 for the first time. Pictured is No. 450099 heading in the opposite direction. (Author)

Below: 'They all look the same to me.' Class 350 EMU No. 350122 pulls into Bescot station in 2021. Fans of EMUs in particular will know of their nuances, which their regular users might not fully appreciate. (Author)

Above and below: The Class 172 is good example of how subclass is important, with the 172/1 and 172/2 having noticeably different cab ends. Pictured is No. 172101 at Kidderminster in Chiltern livery and No. 172216 at Stourbridge Junction. (Author)

Missing out on recognition outside of EMU fans in the south are the withdrawn Class 442 'Plastic Pigs', which once claimed the world speed record for a third-rail train at 109 mph. Pictured is No. 442411 at Brighton railway station in 2012. (Public domain)

Above: Scotland's commuters don't know their luck. The HST sets spread across Britain have dwindled in recent years and the ex-GWR sets run by ScotRail remain a safe haven for enthusiasts of this once groundbreaking train from the 1970s. Pictured is power car No. 43031 leading a train at Kingussie in 2021. (Author)

Right and overleaf top: GWR and CrossCountry HSTs have now all but disappeared from regular service with the introduction of IETs, making scenes like this 2014 picture at Castle Cary confined to history. Two GWR Class 802s are pictured at London Paddington in 2019. (Author)

Also falling by the wayside are the Class 91 hauled services on the East Coast Main Line. Pictured is No. 91132 in GNER livery, at London King's Cross in 2003. (Public domain image by Peter Skuce)

Sleeper services into the Highlands – they play an important part in getting more people to appreciate train travel and perhaps even the trains themselves.

A somewhat bittersweet development in the public's wider enthusiasm for railways has come with the plentiful lines, stations and other pieces of infrastructure that have been abandoned or removed in the last century or earlier. Much is made of the 'Beeching Axe' when it comes to this topic, more accurately described as results of both 'The Reshaping

In Britain, the Settle–Carlisle line is a popular route for travellers, tourists and those pursuing the outdoors from as far as London. It was dubiously threatened with closure in the 1980s but is now thriving with regular and charter traffic and is much loved by enthusiasts, spotters and photographers. Pictured is Class 158 No. 158754 at Settle in 2023. (Author)

A brief distraction from a ski trip in 2018. A PKP Class EN71 waits at Zakopane in Poland, bound for Kraków. (Author)

The Flåm Railway in Norway is featured on many British television programmes, including Channel 5's *World's Most Scenic Railway Journeys*. Tourists flood to lines like this, heading up into the mountains, but for locals they remain a vital lifeline to the rest of their country. Pictured is an NSB El 18 electric locomotive at Flåm in 2023. (Author)

Travelling on commuter lines abroad, such as on Metra Electric running south of Chicago, offers a very different experience for UK enthusiasts. Pictured is a second generation Highliner EMU at University of Chicago/59th St Station in 2022. (Author)

of British Railways' and 'The Development of the Major Railway Trunk Routes' reports of 1963 and 1965 respectively. From the enthusiasts' view, it is brought up with disdain, often tying into nostalgic conversations about the romanticised branch lines of backwater Britain, but in reality, as hard as it might be for some to admit, the resulting public spaces and engaging historic value that footpaths, cycleways, museums and of course heritage railways have offered is of an altogether different, perhaps higher, value than a failing, loss-making part of the national network.

Sustrans National Cycle Route No. 403 runs along most of the former Chippenham and Calne line, which opened in 1863. It was sold to GWR in 1892 and closed by British Rail in 1965. (Author)

A mix of interests can enhance spotting for some. Cromford station in Derbyshire once hosted rock band Oasis for the publicity photograph on their 1995 single *Some Might Say*. Pictured is Class 170 No. 170419 calling there in 2021. (Author)

This is perhaps best demonstrated with the 8.5-mile-long Monsal Trail in Derbyshire, where the former Peak Valley line has been chopped up into various uses to serve a number of different groups. As far as Matlock, the line continues to be run as a branch line serving the likes of Cromford and Matlock Bath, which are both in proximity of worthwhile attractions and amenities for day trippers. At Matlock, Peak Rail run a stretch as a short heritage railway as far as Rowsley and beyond that, between Bakewell and Millers Dale, a series of impressive bridges and tunnels delight thousands of walkers and cyclists, before the line once again sees traffic courtesy of the Great Rocks freight line, which occupies the northern stretch of this former continuous railway line.

Elsewhere, similar stories are told with the early twenty-first century marking a time where both those that remember these lines in operation and those experiencing them for the first time recreationally can converse with one another to allow for an appreciation of these railways by all. Their creation may have been borne of a nightmare for enthusiasts but have become important ways for people to enjoy railways that might not have otherwise materialised.

What has become clear since is that the survival of some lines, even without the rails and stations, has prompted talks over whether they can be resurrected to fulfil today's transport needs. The Peak Valley line is one such line to be earmarked as was the Okehampton branch in Devon, which went from being an occasional weekend summer line, used as a half-heritage, half-main-line railway, to a frequently used part of the GWR network that has renewed relevance for day trippers and hikers wanting easy access to Dartmoor National Park.

Environmental concerns are also seeing more people in the twenty-first century take to domestic train travel for weekend breaks and day trips. This has also contributed to tangible changes in the railway network, such as Okehampton, and has seen a surge in popularity of rural and coastal main-line routes in Scotland, Cornwall and Wales, perhaps muted at times such as the pandemic and during rail strikes. With schemes like emissions charges getting more frequent in Britain's cities (Bristol, Birmingham and Bath being notable additions at the time of writing, with Manchester soon to follow), Park & Ride schemes and

Above and Opposite: Many popular television programmes cover the architecture and structures that the railways necessitated. Liverpool Lime Street station was opened back in 1836 but still serves its function today, as does the iconic Forth Bridge in Scotland. A ScotRail Class 170 *Turbostar* heads towards North Queensferry in 2018. (Author)

Parkway railway stations also receive a renewed relevance, with authorities putting efforts to expand, build and rebuild railway stations and infrastructure in the process.

This gives more people the want or need to travel by train and enthusiasts more railway and more trains to play with, whether out in the field, recreating them at home or simply recording the advancements and changes for prosperity.

5

Spotting and Photography

Train spotting is, in most people's eyes, the most concentrated, serious and purest form that railway enthusiasm can take. It can, in many ways, shroud the appeal of the wider hobby due to negative stereotyping and derogatory association with things such as pedantry or isolation. For decades this arm of rail enthusiasm has been the target of a wholly unnecessary barrage of mocking and beating, at its worst resulting in physical violence but often taking the form of abusive psychological bullying.

Many of those at its heart will in fact attest that spotting is an important part of the history of rail enthusiasm and can be a fulfilling, worthwhile pastime encompassing the outdoors, diligence, patience and determination. This is the reality of spotting and is something that the railway hobby continues to work at in order to shake its unfair reputation among the wider public.

The earliest spotters took pride in seeing the variety of locomotives that worked the British main lines and changed during times when the technology began to advance at a great rate. There continues to be much excitement in seeing the newest locomotives and

Spotters and photographers (author included) congregate at the end of Norton Fitzwarren platform on the West Somerset Railway to see Class 35 D7018. (Author's collection)

Above and previous: Various states of Covid lockdown and restrictions on movement saw the author's first dedicated attempts at trainspotting along the West of England Main Line. Pictured are departmental trains: No. 950001 and the NMT (New Measurement Train) headed by former LNER power car No. 43299 at the abandoned Seaton Junction station. And Colas Rail Class 37 No. 37421 pushing the UTU (Ultrasonic Test Unit) through Axminster, led by DSBO No. 9703 running 3Q07. (Author)

units appearing from the works or arriving from abroad, adding to the vast collection of numbers that an enthusiast might want to spot. Equally there is pleasure, gratification even, in seeing a rare working of something old and outdated. Diesel locomotives from the 1960s and 1970s still commonly work trains up and down the country and steam trains grace the main lines more often than the wider public believe. But though spotting in essence has remained the same branch of the railway hobby over the last century, like other disciplines, the methodology has changed a great deal.

Research and rumour during the twentieth century came largely from those 'in the know'. Efforts between enthusiasts and railway workers would result in a wider dissemination of working timetables, locomotive rosters and short-term planned movements. Publications like the Ian Allen guides became the go-to material for listing class types. Other forms of spotters' books, from the relatively basic 'Eye-Spy' variants to comprehensive and detailed unit number lists, would aid the spotter in collecting and recording the results of their patience. And a great deal of patience was required. Working timetables, in paper format, with little or no indication of whether they were performing to time or not meant that waiting at crossings, stations and bridges formed part of the thrill. Tell-tale signs like the aspect of signals, sounds of level crossing gates or performance of other services would often be the only indication as to whether the intended spot was on its way and even then, the locomotive or unit running the train may well have changed from the original plan.

Highs and lows, elation and disappointment, ensured that this area of the hobby had something of a wider philosophical relationship with the ups and downs that life in general

Internet tools such as Rail Record enabled the author to chase freight for the first time in Lincolnshire. Pictured is Class 60 No. 60100 *Midland Railway – Butterley* at Sleaford, running from Wolverhampton Steel Terminal to Boston Sleaford Sidings. (Author)

Above left and above right: A telephone is available to use at Frinkley Lane level crossing, near Grantham, for those moving livestock or slow vehicles. The stool in the corner may be that of a local spotter or photographer. Approximately 250 trains per day pass here, from the high-speed LNER Azumas and Grand Central Class 180 (pictured) to freight, departmental and rail tour trains. (Author)

can throw at you. On a practical level, the skills involved to be successful at spotting have relevance in many day-to-day tasks and concepts.

Today, the action of spotting remains largely the same. Enthusiasts use timetables and rosters, as well as their own intimate knowledge of the railways, to pick a location of choice, or locomotive of interest – one they 'need' to tick off. Upon arrival, the numbers are noted down, photographs may be taken along with other information that might form a speciality of that particular spotter. This might be carriage formations and numbers, freight cargo, stock movements or locomotive orientation. A unit may have a new nameplate or livery or might be running on a route that's atypical of its standard working. Different spotters spot different things and the best thing about spotting is that there is no right or wrong about what to spot and why.

Spotting is also not as solitary as many might think. There are plenty of photographs and videos online that show gatherings of spotters at stations and on bridges from the 1960s seeing the dying light of the steam age, through to youngsters on platforms during the 1970s playing truant to catch diesel locomotives as they came into service. Contemporary footage often shows groups of spotters lined up at popular venues like Crewe waiting to spot rail tours or freight trains and though they may have travelled many miles to get there, the same familiar faces appear time and time again resulting in light chatter, passionate discussion and generous banter that can only result from a sociable hobby that is strengthened by a collaborative community. In the limited amount of dedicated spotting that the author has done, off-the-cuff conversation with other spotters has been a regular occurrence. A lorry driver on his break at Lincoln snuck in a spot of 'a Class 66 that I've already seen'. And a seasoned spotter at Seaton Junction lamented at the lack of variety from Waterloo and Exeter, the unique departmental Class 950 being the draw for both spotters on that particular day.

What has changed over the course of the last century are the methods for twenty-first-century trainspotting. For a start, safety concerns ensure that responsible spotters remain in areas where they do not pose a danger. As with any hobby like football, skateboarding, nightclubbing or busking, there are those within spotting (a stubborn minority) that bring others into disrepute and spoil it for the rest through reckless actions. Wilful trespassing is perhaps the most obvious, but social media will quickly throw up examples of supposed enthusiasts breaking into cabs during driver breaks, activating alarms, smashing windows and trashing undesirable units during farewell tours. What might have been lighthearted banter between 'Duff' and 'Hoover' bashers during the 1980s has manifested today in teenagers verbally abusing train staff and fellow spotters that prefer certain trains and operators over others.

No one wins from this. As a result, candid access to railway staff, depots, yards and non-public information is harder to come by, meaning that spotters are more and more reliant on the information that is available in the public domain and that which they might share with one another. Some of this restriction is a byproduct of external influences like terrorism, but even acts of irresponsible behavior by those within the railway community give justification to the restrictions on access to the railway itself.

Thankfully, the internet provides a wealth of information, statistics and timetabling to satisfy the needs of many responsible spotters and 'bashers', casual or serious. Services like Rail Record and Realtime Trains offer data not only for commuters and passengers, such as

Above: Being unfamiliar with freight and light engine workings, as well as the notation of internet spotting tools, there was some genuine anticipation for the author at Lincoln, not knowing what would arrive on the Derby RTC to Derby RTC service that was scheduled. Pictured is the answer: Class 20s No. 20205 and No. 20227 *Sherlock Holmes* in BR blue and London Transport liveries respectively. (Author)

Below: At Bescot, where 'Harry' Williams was said to have moved freight during the Second World War, GBRf Class 66 No. 66771 and No. 66709 top-and-tail a new weedkilling system, having tested it on the nearby Severn Valley Railway. (Author)

Class 66s, known colloquially as 'sheds', might be looked down upon by spotters from a time with vast varieties of traction, but their versatility sees them on many different workings. Here, No. 66743 in Belmond livery waits to depart Kingussie while passengers enjoy fine dining in 2021. (Author)

seat availability, live tracking and service information, but also the rostered unit/locomotive numbers, planned diversions and the nature of the train – is it freight, is it engineering, is it a rail tour or light engine movement? Some of these services are interactive. Rail Record allows for users to log in and record the locomotive/unit numbers of a set service in real time, so that other users can see what's coming. A spotter at Birmingham New Street might record a CrossCountry service featuring a Class 43 HST set, such that someone waiting in Taunton might be able to see it and time their wait in the area around its arrival, thus ignoring any other services featuring Voyagers, which for many have less of a spotting value.

Below and opposite: Crewe station provides a veritable feast of diesel and electric units to spot from multiple operators, as well as freight trains and rail tours. Pictured within an hour in July 2023 are: TfW Class 175 No. 175003, Freightliner Class 66 No. 66570, Northern Class 323 No. 323229 and TfW Class 150 No. 150267. (Author)

Social media more widely impacts on spotting both with the spreading of real-time information and the general 'hype' surrounded by an increasingly vocal railway hobby following. With a large and growing community of railfans and enthusiasts eager to post on Facebook, Twitter/X, Instagram and more recently TikTok, other spotters can engage from behind the keyboard both proactively and negatively with one another. Spotters might go out based on what they've seen someone else post from a location, or simply relish in an expert bit of video footage obtained from someone many miles from where they're based. On occasion, a wider non-enthusiast audience, even celebrities or the press, might begin to react to a post from a passionate spotter, or to some exciting railway footage of something with wider appeal, like LNER Class A3 *Flying Scotsman*.

This has perhaps come to light most notably with the rise of Luke Nicolson, known to most as social media sensation and trainspotter Francis Bourgeois. His whimsical exaggeration of his genuine passion and knowledge of trains has been something the author has experienced firsthand. The internet has questioned his authenticity, given the lucrative and opportunistic dealings he has had with the likes of Gucci, music stars, footballers and main-line TOCs, but while he has perhaps attracted this criticism through reasonable suspicion and a degree of jealously in the railway community, his enthusiasm for trains and railways is most certainly authentic and has done more good to the hobby than harm in recent years.

This reluctance by some to see the hobby thrive exemplifies a trope that is common among a minority of enthusiasts of all ages and backgrounds – selfishness. Many believe that the hobby, and particularly their knowledge of it, is theirs and theirs alone. Competition thrives in discussion with some enthusiasts, all eager to point out the errors of others rather than collaborating and rejoicing in the ability to teach and nurture knowledge amongst them. In larger settings, projects, initiatives and even funding that would benefit a wider group of enthusiasts and followers can be withheld and protected by one individual either for vanity, recognition or through sheer spite. Entities like Francis Bourgeois do much to snuff out this attitude by being so open and candid with the wider public.

Internet forums also provide a more concentrated outlet for spotters and enthusiasts to share their progress and discuss various topics relevant to their passion. Here, a more dedicated contingent of the internet-savvy enthusiast often exists, discussing anything from the political impact of HS2 on the future of railways, to the freshest livery given to a certain locomotive. The passing down of information and sharing of knowledge once confined to memory and notepads can be forever recorded in endless forum threads, from the running of a rare but regular interloper service, to the reasons behind some trains being restricted on certain routes and the likelihood of some units ever seeing service again. If an enthusiast has a burning question, often asking the internet can result in finding the answer through forums populated by more experienced enthusiasts and railway staff.

But as with most subjects on the internet, much hostility can arise, and arguments can cause tension within the enthusiast community. Casual or young enthusiasts can be derided by the 'old guard' and immature enthusiasts can disrespect those with greater experience and knowledge. The pedantry and pettiness that the general public often associate with the railway hobby gets plastered across the internet publicly, resulting in further confusion and mocking of what can be a wonderful pastime. While this issue permeates most hobbies – football, Formula 1, gaming and Harry Potter forums can be just as divisive and off-putting – arguments and bickering among railway enthusiasts over the validity of 9351 or yellow safety panel placement on a Class 92 sadly add fuel to a century-old fire that sees rail enthusiasts, and spotters specifically, derided by the masses.

At its worst, things like racism and misogyny can creep into this realm, particularly with generational divides, and the hobby can be spoiled by a lack of unity among spotters and other enthusiast communities.

This shouldn't take away from the fact that the internet has made spotting much more accessible to a much wider group of people. While purists might argue that the use of more technology takes away the unpredictability of a hobby that instilled so much drama and discipline for spotters, what they can't deny is that it makes the hobby much more efficient and open. The wealth of information online also brings more people to the hobby, from the young tech-savvy enthusiasts embarking on their first solo spot, to the older or less-able spotters, confined to their homes. Railcam services on YouTube allow people to spot from home; this was particularly relevant during the Covid-19 pandemic, when trains were running but people were less able to move around the country.

On the railways themselves, the current but ever-changing fleet of units and locomotives gives spotters a plethora of things to spot up and down the country. There are those whose goal it is to spot every Class 66 locomotive – a reasonable task made possible through their ability to work on most parts of the network. Others may be bored with their local line, perhaps a branch line frequented only by the same type of multiple unit (or in some cases the same unit) and instead wish to see what the rest of the country has to offer. And the casual spotters, of which the author is one, may take a more holistic approach – whatever comes, comes, with number taking being of little consequence at all.

Photography on the other hand, while closely linked to spotting, is a different discipline altogether. Whether purely a railway photographer or someone with a more varied commercial repertoire, some of the skills required for enthusiasts getting into railway photography marry with those of spotting – research, tracking and patience among them.

But unlike spotting, railway photography can be big business and has been a financially viable outlet for the hobby since the publication of some of the first railway magazines. Wider news stories about historic railway milestones, *Flying Scotsman*, rail strikes and sadly even rail accidents all provide mainstream media with the need for the existence of railway photographers, whether they capture contemporary industry-led photos, or those related to heritage railways or main-line rail tours. Within the rail enthusiast community, there is equal appetite for seeing trains captured in the best way possible.

Like spotting and to a lesser extent modelling, social media has transformed the way photographs are viewed and shared. Photo-centric platforms like Instagram are apt outlets for amateur and professional railway photographers with some garnering many hundreds of thousands of followers from within and beyond rail enthusiasm. Trains and locomotives are seen at their best by millions of people across the world, allowing trains from one region to be seen and enjoyed by those whom otherwise might not ever see them in the flesh. In some cases, railway photographers can make a good earning on selling their output to enthusiasts directly, much in the way other types of photographers do, in sport, politics or show business. Those pursuing the same targets on the rails could easily attract the moniker 'Railway Paparazzi'.

Above: Sometimes the scenery is as important as the train. An unidentified First Great Western HST runs through rural Somerset in September 2014. (Author)

Below: Like any form of photography, railway photography can be an important record of the landscape and its history. The scene at Didcot Parkway, pictured in 2013, has since lost the iconic cooling towers from the adjacent power station. Class 66 No. 66067 is stabled to the right of picture. (Author)

Railways and their infrastructure set into the wider landscape make for interesting backdrops and vistas for photographers. Pictured is a Chiltern Railways Class 168 No. 168004 with Wembley Stadium in the background in 2018. (Author)

Above left and above right: Beyond stock imagery and personal photographs of non-enthusiasts, train interiors are not often taken, seen or shared largely to maintain privacy of passengers. This empty Virgin Trains *Pendolino* service in 2014 provides an opportunity to do so, though why this image was taken, the author cannot remember.

Class 390 *Pendolinos* were later taken on by Avanti West Coast, as depicted here at Lea Hall in 2023. (Author)

The accessibility of camera technology also has a profound effect on the coverage of trains on social media. Almost everyone, whether they're a railway enthusiast or not, will have a high-quality camera built into their phone in this century, with editing tools often accompanying them. Filters and zoom make capturing appealing photographs very easy with mobile coverage and WiFi making sharing them just as simple. The internet sees these images published instantaneously and 'live' in synergy with the information distributed by spotters. In the twenty-first century, while not everyone can become a high-quality, professional railway photographer, almost anyone can photograph a train.

Above: Rail tours attract spotters and photographers with varying degrees of interest, including photographers with no specific knowledge of trains. Pictured are two Class 47s on a diesel rail tour snaking towards Clysthayes Bridge, Devon, in 2021. (Author)

Opposite above: Like on heritage railways, steam rail tours attract more attention on the main line. Pictured at Norton Fitzwarren arriving onto the West Somerset Railway is LMS Jubilee Class No. 45596 *Bahamas* in 2021. (Author)

In the United States, Roger Puta (1944–90) is perhaps one of the most notable railway photographers. Much of his collection is available online and in the public domain coutesy of Mel Finzer and Marty Bernard's Flickr account. Pictured is *Flying Scotsman* at Glenndale, MD, on 25 October 1969. (A Roger Puta photograph)

6

Railway Simulation

Perhaps the most conclusive way in which twenty-first-century technology has impacted and grown the railway hobby is through interactive simulation and video games. Cars, sports, planes and other areas of enthusiasm were quick to jump on the growth of the video game industry since it exploded in the 1980s, but trains have been slower to make use of the platform, perhaps due to the discrimination against enthusiasts that was widespread at the time. Today, however, it has very much caught up, with the latest train simulation games offering something far beyond the more casual but popular racing and combat titles.

This area of the hobby itself has a number of different off-shoots suiting a wide variety of those interested in railways. Earlier train-centric games like *Railway Tycoon* gave players the ability to run a railway, with the accuracy of rolling stock, history and geography of little consequence – the world is yours to build and grow. Others centred more on the way railways fit into a wider transport or settlement setting. The *Sim City* (and more recent *City Skylines*) series have featured ways in which to implement railways into an urban landscape, impacting on the way that industry and residential districts win or lose and how trade impacts with adjacent cities and territories. But while these often give a top-down view (quite literally in some cases) of railways as a whole, perhaps the most relevant genre for rail enthusiasts is that of train simulation – operating and driving the trains themselves.

Leading this area is Dovetail Games, the trading name for RailSimulator.com Ltd. Since the first iteration of their ongoing train simulation franchises, *RailWorks*, released in 2009, the company has grown to create video games for both PC and console users (PlayStation and Xbox) that place the player in the cab of a vast array of British, American and European rolling stock as they run through faithfully recreated environments representing a variety of different time periods. The detail and dedication that their team put into these titles, now under the *Train Sim World* and *Train Simulator Classic* banners, has resulted in a hobby in itself and an associated community. Train simulation is akin in many ways to the modelling hobby in terms of costs, collectability and the time required to nurture further skill and interest.

This has led to some push back on the hobby, most notably by traditionalist modellers claiming that video games as a whole have been killing the more analogue pastimes of board games, modelling and outdoor pursuits. But this has never been the intention of most video games developers in the railway space. Dovetail Games, who proudly state that their products are made 'By Enthusiasts, For Enthusiasts' employ a large number of enthusiasts that themselves model, spot and photograph on the railways. A healthy combination of these hobbies is often seen, with one building on the interest of another. And their intention is to ensure that their players do the same.

As a result of its popularity and accessibility, particularly with younger audiences, competition is rife among the railway simulation video game genre. Other ventures like *SimRail* have experimented with multiplayer features, allowing enthusiasts to play with one another. Others like *Derail Valley* forego accuracy and licensed branding for engaging gameplay and puzzle solving. Casual enthusiasts may want to build trains or destroy them, rather than simulate them in high detail. Over the last decade, trains have become playable in formats catering for those whom have little interest in locomotives and history, as well as those at the heart of the hobby, for whom detail and accuracy is everything. Catering for both gamers and rail enthusiasts is a balancing act that companies have to consider when making a video game in this genre.

More importantly, simulators give people of all interests an appreciation for the day-to-day of those that currently or formerly operated trains. The difficulty and complexity of the cab, whether steam, diesel or electric, can come across so perfectly in some cases that those whom never had the chance to go into the railway industry themselves can finally

Pictured at the East Lancashire Railway's Buckley Wells Depot in 2022, the Class 40 Preservation Society once hosted a mobile simulator, complete with cab from No. 40008, which was salvaged when it was scrapped at Crewe in 1988. (Author)

Above and below: *Train Simulator Classic* has been around for over a decade, building on the same fundamentals each year with thousands of add-ons made by both Dovetail Games and third-party developers. The latter form a cottage industry of its own, covering trains from many nations and eras. Pictured are unbranded iterations of the Class 360 and Class 175. (Screenshot from *Train Simulator Classic*, ©2023 Dovetail Games)

Train Sim World utilises the power of Unreal Engine to display trains and environments in a great amount of detail for both PC and console players. British content is well represented, as shown here in *Train Sim World 4*'s Training Center. *Left* to right: plain-liveried Class 323, LMS 8F and Class 66. (Screenshot from *Train Sim World*®, ©2023 Dovetail Games)

take control of trains in a virtual setting. Opportunities like this can only otherwise be found through costly real-world driver courses on heritage railways, which are for many prohibitive not only on cost but require certain levels of physical strength and mental awareness. Train simulators give players the chance to make mistakes, press buttons and generally do things that might otherwise have never been done on a railway in a similar manner to some of the more fantastical arrangements seen in the model railway world.

At times when the relevance and value of train drivers is questioned in the media, these simulators also provide perspective for the masses on how important the analogue person at the controls is to the operational safety and punctuality of train services. Like all railway hobbies, they also provide impetus for those getting into the railway industry themselves. A gaming interest today is no less relevant than a modelling interest was when recruiting for the big railway decades ago and a crossover between the main line and video games industries has begun to emerge.

7

Employment and the Industry

It should be stated, before getting into how railway enthusiasm and railway employment work with one another today, that though the author has worked within the railway hobby for over a decade and worked full time for a heritage railway, that they have not (yet) embarked on any main line or contemporary railway industry work. However, a great deal of insight comes from acquaintances and colleagues leading to the conclusion that progression into the rail industry from the hobby is something that regularly occurs. This is the opposite of what might have occurred during the last century, where employment on the railways naturally resulted in enthusiasm in later life.

At the various heights of railway activity during Britain's past, working on the railways was as necessary and important as those working today in the NHS or in supermarkets – being involved in an area of life that had relevance for almost everyone, almost every day. Many people joining the industry may not have had much interest in trains or locomotives, but as their fledgling jobs became lifelong careers, spanning the advancements outlined earlier, their enthusiasm into retirement would have forged their hobby and interest beyond the hours of their shifts. Whether at home on the model railway layout, or forming part of the local preservation movement, the outlet of passion for railways stemmed from their time working on them.

All in a day's work. Staff observe Class 08 No. 08798 approaching a Pathfinder Tours rail tour at Swansea East Dock to replace a Class 47 in November 1989. (Richard Szwejkowski)

Today, though this almost certainly repeats itself for those that find their way into the industry, it is also true that the opposite can occur, where an initial interest and enthusiasm for railways can eventually raise a keen interest in working for them full time. For those born post-preservation movement, heritage railways are an incredibly important part of this process, not only sparking inspiration in a childhood imagination that might one day materialise in an application with a main-line operator, but also in providing employment opportunities themselves in the areas of commercial tourism, marketing and restoration

Above: Westbury is a hive of activity for passenger, freight and other unusual trains, as well as shunting. Here a member of the 'orange army' is seen approaching a stationary Class 66 No. 66053 in 2021. (Author)

Right: Previous to that, shunting was performed by the seemingly invulnerable Class 08 shunter. This example, No. 08799 *Fred*, is pictured in 2014. (Author)

among others. Learning the processes and terminology of the railway world in a casual environment like a heritage railway can give some people a headstart when competing for positions with main-line operators and companies.

The Chartered Institution of Railway Operators (CIRO) recently opened up affiliate membership to volunteers on some heritage railways, which the author duly took up. This provided access to a host of courses, social events and qualifications which could (if desired) provide an ample platform for going directly from the hobby and preservation arm of railways into the main-line industry. Indeed, their Introduction to Rail course has been specifically

Left: Permenant way gangs and track engineers form an often unsung contingent of the railway industry's workforce, but enthusiasts both recognise and appreciate their efforts. Railway Tampers have their own specific following. Pictured is Colas Rail Matisa B41UE Tamper DR75406 *Eric Machell* at Tiverton Loop. (Author)

Below: Delays due to 'leaves on the line' have become the butt of jokes for passengers, but are a serious matter in the industry. RHTTs (Railhead Treatment Trains) are employed during autumnal months to combat this, sometimes facilitated by locomotives. Pictured are GBRf Class 69 Nos 69001 and 69002 with an RHTT at Gillingham, Kent. (Author)

aimed at those coming into the railways from other industries and backgrounds, for example a social media manager who may have come from an unrelated industry like hospitality.

Simulation has had a say here too to some degree, with the accuracy of more recent examples on popular gaming consoles inspiring individuals to apply for driver training courses and use their basic knowledge of railway operations gleaned through hours of video gaming to contribute to efficiency and success of both main line and heritage railways.

The railway hobby is itself an industry, though it is not often thought of as one. All the disciplines mentioned in previous chapters have their own employment opportunities, whether it be modelling, photography, tourism or even video games, giving people the chance to share and expand their passions to greater audiences, while making a living in an area that they can more often than not enjoy. It is this industry in which the author finds himself, having once been the wide-eyed child on the platform at Tywyn or Kidderminster in the 1990s. Others have no doubt done the same.

But the funnel that the hobby creates for the mainstream railway industry is also important, providing a steady flow of willing, fresh talent to take up the station duties,

Above left and above right: A view seldom seen by the public. Right is the view from the fireman's position out towards the boiler of GWR Large Prairie steam locomotive No. 5199, with left being the driver's position in the cab of Electric Multiple Unit AM9/Class 309 No. 309624. (Author)

answer the ticketing enquiries and even enter the cab as a result of the knowledge and enthusiasm that they've shown over many years with railways as a hobby. Like other industries, this injection of dedicated individuals is what can ensure a safe and happy future for main-line TOCs, Network Rail and more profoundly in areas where senior decisions are made, like in government. The input that enthusiasts can have by working with those outside the railway sphere can be incredibly important.

Enthusiasts dream of the day that they get to view a bonafide main-line rail depot. For many, this is as close as they will get. Class 377 No. 377521 and Class 466 No. 466032 sit at Gillingham EMUD in March 2022. The fence runs along the pavement of Ingram Road, allowing for safe, legal shots such as this. Both classes are far outweighed in number by the closely related Class 375 and 465. (Author)

Freight is a largely misunderstood arm of railway operation that few members of the public get to truly appreciate. Though the UK utilises freight trains far less than the United States and Europe, their presence is important. A colourful array of containers is pictured here heading south from Bescot in the West Midlands. (Author)

8

Other Arms of the Hobby

As with any hobby, a great deal of smaller but no less passionate offshoots grow out of the want to take an individual or group interest in a very specific direction. Some of these remain isolated and hidden by the much larger scope of things like spotting and modelling, whereas others breakthrough to form considerable hobbies of their own, often with attitudes that differ noticeably from the more mainstream areas of railway enthusiasm.

The Moors Valley Railway near Ringwood, Hampshire, is one of the most impressive 7¼-inch-gauge miniature railways in Britain. Like the Beer Heights Light Railway in Devon, it is approximately 1 mile in length, but traverses bridges, threads through tunnels and stops at two stations in the wider country park. (Author)

The author enjoys a rare experience as driver on his last day working as Assistant Site Manager at Pecorama, home of the Beer Heights Light Railway, in 2017. The locomotive is *Dickie*, delivered in 1976 just one year after the attraction was first opened by modelling company PECO. (Author's collection)

One of these notable areas is that of miniature railways. Sometimes described as garden railways, these ride-on constructs are scattered across Britain in a variety of locations and settings, ranging from private railways shielded permanently from public view, to small attractions within wider country park or stately home settings and at the extreme end, sizeable tourist attractions in their own right. Generally considered to be railways with a gauge of less than 15 inches, these private follies, built and financed often by landowners and eccentric enthusiasts, cropped up largely at the start of the twentieth century but have ebbed and flowed in the subsequent decades, with some closing, some reopening, some moving location and others being built from scratch into this century.

Though many of those that own, run and work on these railways and locomotives have a significant crossover of interests with mainstream railway enthusiasts, the same cannot be said for the inverse. Seen by some as whimsical toys with little historic or otherwise technical railway value, the miniature railway hobby has to hold its own with a strong community across its varying gauges dealing with the maintenance and production of miniature locomotives as well as the running of their many locations and organising of events both for those within that community and the wider general public.

Observers of this community will quickly note the freedom of mindset and lack of pedantry that those within it express. Though some of the bigger concerns like the Beer Heights Light Railway in Devon and Moors Valley Railway in Hampshire have complex signalling, multiple stations and entire fleets of steam, diesel and battery electric locomotives, their want for visiting engines, changes to layouts and running methods and interest in receiving custom from predominantly families and young children, set them apart from more stringently operated heritage railways and the rules and regulations that govern them. This attitude makes their environment very welcoming to newcomers and with ownership of both railways and locomotives within financial means for those with modest savings, pensions and expendable income, this miniature hobby has more in common with the likes of classic car ownership than that of railway enthusiasts.

Though some full-scale railway enthusiasts may dismiss miniature railways as follies or toys, the locomotives are no less technically impressive than engines of larger size. Conversely, miniature railway hobbyists are often more relaxed and open to a wider scope of the railway hobby. Pictured is the privately owned *Otter* in the Beer Heights Light Railway workshop. (Author)

The Romney, Hythe & Dymchurch Railway in Kent is one of the most popular light railways in Britain, running up to 25 mph on 15-inch-gauge track. Though now a tourist venture, it was opened as a passenger railway in 1927 and has a notable military past. It was ultimately the passion project of two wealthy enthusiasts: Captain 'Jack' Howey and Count Louis Zborowski. Pictured is 1925 locomotive *Green Goddess* at Dungeness station in 2022. (Author)

Passionate followers of the London Underground also sit apart from the general railway enthusiast. Again, though there might be some crossover in interest between the two, the specific history, rolling stock and operations centred around London's wider transport network necessitate its own dedicated enthusiasts that are responsible for supporting the likes of Covent Garden's London Transport Museum, the depot at Acton and the running of preserved stock along the present network much in the way that heritage rail tours continue

Stationary engines, like traction engines, arguably have little to do with railways, but the enthusiasm for them is similar. At Westonzoyland Pumping Station in Somerset, the disarming charm and noted lack of pedantry sees families, locals, agricultural and history enthusiasts gather comfortably in one place. The Westonzoyland Light Railway pictured bears little resemblance culturally to a heritage railway. (Author)

to do on the main line. Though fans of the London Underground might seem to concentrate on a very specific set of lines and trains, their hobby in fact encompasses interest in a much wider set of topics, often crossing paths with the wider transport enthusiasts (including trams and buses) and capturing the hearts and minds of an international audience given the recognition that 'the Tube' has across the globe. Seldom would a member of the public wear clothing adorned with LMS or LNER branding, whereas millions of tourists seek solace in the various logos and motifs owned by TfL.

Signalling might initially seem like an integral part of the railway hobby, and it is certainly true that many enthusiasts have rudimentary knowledge of signalling practice. But this dark art, described once to the author as a railway 'language', results in confined projects started up by those that have dedicated experience within this area. Exeter West Signal Box (now at Crewe Heritage Centre) has, on operating days, its own simulated timetable giving volunteers in the 'box a taste of an entire day's work pulling the various levers and ringing bells in the correct sequence to correctly signal a section of railway as per the 1960s. Similar projects at Swindon Panel (at the Didcot Railway Centre) and Romsey are in place thanks to those with a specific interest in this area.

As alluded to earlier, entities like Thomas the Tank Engine gave rise to groups of enthusiasts that dedicate their time specifically to it. Comprised of many that would be considered twenty-first-century enthusiasts, this fandom perhaps has a closer relationship with those of Marvel movies and Star Wars than that of other arms of the railway hobby. In

Above: The London Underground has a following consisting of former staff, London eccentrics, historians, transport enthusiasts and rail enthusiasts, but crossovers are not always a given and some followers know little of railways beyond Greater London. Pictured at Putney Bridge in 2022 is a District Line S7 Stock Underground train. (Author)

Right: The Isle of Wight is where London Underground and main-line railway worlds collide. Though the Class 483 units (formerly 1938 stock – pictured in 2011 at Smallbrook Junction) have been removed from there, their Class 484 replacements are themselves modernised and modified D78 stock once seen on the District line. (Author)

online forums and social media, fans of the series conjure up their own backstories for its cast of characters, create their own personas in the form of a named locomotive (complete with appearance and characteristics indicative of its creator) and write their own fan fiction, taking the adventures of established characters and their own off into wild tangents and places, from real life locations and railways (including heritage railways) to the universes occupied by other popular fiction series like *Doctor Who*. Like other seemingly

For some, carriages and wagons are of more interest than locomotives and units. Some heritage railways have separate groups dedicated to carriages, brake vans or industrial rolling stock. Freshly repainted in 2021 are two maroon Mk 1 coaches at Minehead station. (Author)

Historic road vehicles, from cars to buses, have a much wider appeal to casual and serious motoring enthusiasts of all backgrounds and ages and this openness is candidly experienced at places such as Transport Museum, Wythall, just outside of Birmingham. (Author)

Above left: Furnicular railway enthusiasm is largely unheard of, but travellers and fans of these steep, peculiar tourist traps love to make the most of them and their history. Pictured is the Lynton & Lynmouth Cliff Railway in Devon, in 2019. (Author)

Above right: *Thomas the Tank Engine* was a childhood favourite of the author (pictured), though unlike many of today's fans, he did not find the series appealing into adolescence or adulthood. The book and television series undoubtedly inspired a generation of railway enthusiasts. (Author's collection)

innocent pop culture brands and phenomena, there are even those who place an adult twist on the series, resulting in some bizarre and distasteful crossover material.

When talking about offshoots of the railway hobby, it is also relevant to mention the interest that British enthusiasts have in railways beyond the confines of the United Kingdom. British railway enthusiasts find a great deal of interest in railways abroad, whether that be because companies like BREL, English Electric and Brush Traction once exporting a number of locomotives and units beyond the UK, with some preserved. Or because of the vast differences with rolling stock that nations in Europe and America have in size, power, use and style of operation. As well as the benefit of inspiring rail enthusiasts to travel abroad, understanding foreign railways also casts a light on the differing attitudes elsewhere. In some nations, 'railfanning' is far less restricted, under the assumption that most will be sensible enough not to trespass or act unlawfully around railway lines. In others, such staunch support of one discipline is frowned upon. The steam/diesel divide, for example, is noticeably less divisive in the United States, where railfans seem to be happy embracing railways as a whole, rather than arguing for a certain faction of their hobby.

Enthusiasts keen on a certain theme or style might gain more from exploring beyond Britain, such as those passionate about locomotive haulage. Swiss railways have a keen British following because of their ageing electric locomotives, having been some of the first on the rails owing to a lack of coal and liquid fuel in isolated mountain regions and the nearby use of hydroelectric power.

There are many more sub-hobbies, offshoots and derivatives of the vast railway hobby, each with their own vast collections of knowledge, challenges, communities and opposers, but perhaps now more than ever do they have the recognition, support and validity that allow them to thrive as peripheral components of the wider railway hobby. They form crucial parts of railway enthusiasm as a whole in the UK.

Above: Northern Ireland's railways and rolling stock get considerably less attention in the British railway hobby. Pictured is a sorry looking NIR 80 Class DMU power car No. 8099 at the East Lancashire Railway in 2022, thought to be preserved solely to provide spares for English 'Thumper' units. (Author)

Opposite: The author unexpectedly overhears a group of British rail enthusiasts gathering unit and locomotive numbers in Cologne, Germany, in 2023. Locomotive haulage has dwindled greatly in the UK since the year 2000, with native enthusiasts exploring other nations to see the same variety of workings as in previous decades. Pictured is DB BR 146 No. 146003 at Cologne at the rear of a push-pull service to Aachen Hauptbahnhof. (Author)

Similarly, the United States continues to use diesel locomotives built decades ago. Left is Metra's F40PH 145 *City of Aurora* built in 1980 and right is UP Y723, a GP15-1 locomotive built in 1982. Both are performing passenger and switching duties respectively at Chicago's Ogilvie Transportation Center in 2022. (Author)

9

Inclusivity: A Hobby for All?

There's no point in avoiding the fact that for many decades the railway hobby has been largely male dominated. An entirely separate work may be written – should be written – in future about where this stemmed from and how this came to be. An obvious answer lies within the wider stance that society took over previous centuries and millennia. This work would require input from someone with a clear finger on the pulse of the many controversial and sensitive topics that would surround it and though we all have a responsibility to be mindful of this, it would not be right for the author to be the authoritative voice on this matter. Such a work would hopefully conclude that in the twenty-first century significant progress has been made to ensure that everyone has an opportunity to join the railway hobby and that the hobby is in a much better place as a result.

Recent years have proven that the heritage railway sector has much to learn on this matter. The East Lancashire Railway became embroiled in controversy when sacking a

Open access. A scene at Ebbw Vale from May 1987 shows how things have changed for the enthusiast over the last fifty years. Onlookers, majority male, wander the tracks freely around Class 40 No. 40122 and its train. Despite less physical access to the railway, access generally to the hobby is more open today than ever before. (Richard Szwejkowski)

female member of footplate crew over their complaints around sexism, and the extensive thoughts and accounts shared online by a West Somerset Railway volunteer shed light on the negative and wildly offensive attitudes of those at high levels in heritage railways around transgender people. There is, quite simply, no reason for the railway hobby and industry to restrict its scope of followers to one gender.

Though publicised considerably less, perhaps the next biggest area of discrimination within heritage railways in particular surrounds that of young people and a lack of willingness for older, established personnel to accept the input of new blood. In its worst form this can result in bullying, grooming and shrouding the successes of young volunteers by having their older superiors take credit for their efforts. In more a common form, many younger people simply don't have the confidence to get involved at all.

The simple reality of all railway hobby disciplines is that none need to be limited to one specific group of people. There is no reason at all for any one area to work against or rule out a certain group of people, whether that be on account of ethnicity, gender, sexual orientation, physical or mental ability or age. Trains, locomotives and the railways as a whole can, and should, be enjoyed by anyone and there are many ways that the hobby adapts to positively include as many people as possible.

Leading by example, in many ways, is the main-line industry. On a practical level, so much of the network is now accessible for wheelchair users and those with less visible disabilities. While this is largely with the accommodation of more passengers in mind, the ability for this to open up the hobby to those concerned is just as important, allowing hobbyists access to platforms, footbridges and trains so that they might see, hear and experience railways that are local to them.

Equally, employment practice has opened up the industry to a much more diverse range of people, with more women, people from ethnic minority groups and LGBTQ+ representation visible in a large range of roles. This opens up the hobby to others in those groups, seeing that there are like-minded individuals to engage with, work with and talk

Lumo's 'Pride Partnerships' train, Class 803 No. 803003, echoing many similar initiatives across the network to promote inclusivity and support for LGBTQ+ communities both in and out of the railway industry. (Angus Duncan)

to, along with those from different groups that are open and inclusive. Many public-facing initiatives have driven this change to a more open railway society, most notably with the introduction of multiple Trainbow locomotives and units on the network, keenly spotted by many enthusiasts due to their unique liveries and names. Vocal personalities in these areas, from Tim Dunn and Geoff Marshall to Katie Price and her son Harvey, have also done a great deal to talk about railways in the context of making them available for everyone.

However, there's always more that can be done, particularly with heritage railways. While some of the more commercially astute examples have successfully positioned themselves as more open and inclusive, many others fail dismally to 'read the room' and either make efforts to distance themselves from what they see as a 'woke agenda' or enact superficial change as a box-ticking exercise without any tangible impact on the accessibility of either their railway or railways generally. While spotting, travelling on and enjoying the main-line railway has become notably more open and available, along with modelling to a degree, the heritage railway sector is perhaps one area where the attitudes of old have not yet allowed for this positive change.

Solutions to improving this situation will always cause division and a difference in opinion. But when the goal is to make railways more accessible to everyone, there shouldn't be any logical or sensible reason to argue against it. The more people coming into the railway hobby, from a more diverse range of society, the better that the hobby will be.

Terminology has adapted in more recent times to be more inclusive. Armsbands formerly identifying 'pilotman' now simply say 'pilot'. Similarly, 'signalman' is more commonly changed to 'signaller', with the increasing presence of female and non-binary staff and hobbyists. (Author's collection)

10

The Future of the Hobby

Writing about the future of the railway hobby is incredibly difficult as no one can predict the future. Indeed, if the intended publication window is accurate, some topics talked about here will have advanced quite significantly by the time this book hits the shelves.

What's perhaps even harder is avoiding a bias towards the negative, particularly in times when the world seems at odds with itself in so many areas and something like the passion for trains becomes arguably insignificant. Each area of the hobby will undoubtedly face its own challenges in years to come, whether it be the use of plastic in modelling, the cost of running a heritage railway or the use of main-line diesel locomotives in an environmental context. Like many things, railway enthusiasts must adapt to survive and those that refuse to might see themselves disadvantaged in the future.

We've already seen this in so many areas. Those that live in the past, rather than remembering it fondly, lie at the heart of current conflicts between steam and diesel, young and old, analogue and digital. In time, those reluctant to accept change and greet newcomers to the hobby with open arms will be responsible for the death of all that's great about railways. The more, the merrier. The merrier, the healthier.

But those who do rejoice in the ever-changing landscape of Britain's railway network and pastimes have much to look forward to. Technology ever advances. Rolling stock

The fate of many items of rolling stock today. A goods van sits on a private site in Somerset awaiting conversion into a shepherd's hut. Many such vans and wagons can be seen on farms in the county and beyond used as storage sheds, chicken coops and lucrative Airbnb venues. (Author)

The former Sandford and Banwell station in Somerset now forms part of the Sandford Station Retirement Village, with residents able to look out at the platform, occupied by a static display Sentinel Works No. 9387, two wagons and a Mk 1 carriage. The station is open on certain days throughout the year. Perhaps more of these sites will develop to please ageing railway enthusiasts of the future. (Author)

books and railway magazines, whether digital or in print, will expand into areas anew. Battery-powered EMUs might soon grace lines without third rails or OHLE and shunting locomotives with battery technology, including input from Tesla, have seen trials in yards. One such example used that ubiquitous locomotive, the Class 08, as the basis for its project, which resulted in the unveiling of the striking Class 08e.

Hydrogen might make an appearance in either multiple unit or locomotive format, though the planned conversion of Class 321 units seems to have gone quiet. And while the death of the locomotive seems a foregone conclusion to many, technology might yield the opposite, with the latest orders of the newest Class 93 still to arrive at the time of writing. There might even be an end for the Class 66, with GBRf ordering a fleet of Class 99 locomotives (not to be confused with the TOPS designation for British Rail's train ferries) that are planned to replace them on freight services. Exciting things are no doubt to come when it comes to advancing traction.

Heritage railways may also not be so concerned. The fewer antiquities that exist on the main line, the more that might become viable for preservation. In those outfits that truly care for the saving of important items for the appreciation of future generations, a barrage of rolling stock and historical items may soon be on their way to museums and societies up and down the nation. With efforts to preserve relevant items comes funding and support from both the public and beyond. Of those heritage lines connected to the main line, the prospect of takeover might be doom and gloom, but what better way to justify the preservation of a railway line than to have it reopen for main-line traffic, thus once

Prototype Class 230 Vivarail D-Train, formerly London Underground D78 stock, calls at a temporary platform at Long Marston during Rail Live 2017. Battery operated trains, or BEMUs, are seen to be the future on some branch lines. (Public domain image by Spsmiler)

The Elizabeth Line recently invigorated an interest among the wider public for modern rail transport within London. Pictured here is a Class 345 Aventra at Abbey Wood in 2023. (Author)

New traction keeps appearing. By the time of publication these new Class 196 Civity DMUs, pictured here at Wellington (Shropshire) station, will have been in service for a few years. (Author)

again serving its community, its people and its enthusiasts with or without its heritage stock? Are heritage railways babysitting for a future of reconnecting with the network? A controversial idea no doubt, but one that may one day require more serious deliberation. Indeed, the seeds have already been sewn in some parts. Offshoot organisations in and around (and sometimes in conflict with) some heritage lines are making use of government conversations relevant to public transport funding and reopening initiatives to bring regular running services to the Wensleydale, Weardale, East Lancashire and West Somerset Railways with varying degrees of progress.

As for the people themselves – us, the enthusiasts – the way we interact with the world is paramount to our future. Social media is here to stay, along with all things internet and advancing technology. Already it is clear that on the whole these things enhance the shareability, accessibility, popularity and (in many cases) profitability of the hobby. Photographers and videographers will have more at their disposal to share and communicate their work to others; spotters will be able to 'tick off' their targets more quickly and efficiently; modellers will build better, more impressive and more accurate layouts, with products that integrate more devices than ever before and simulators will continue to bring people into the cabs of iconic locomotives and environments.

Yet more lines are planned to reopen. At the time of writing, the Portishead branch line near Bristol has not been reopened but may well have been by the time of publication. Pictured is the former Portbury railway station, with old rails still in situ back in March 2014. (Author)

And the railways themselves? In essence they shall remain as they have been for almost 200 years. Parallel rails connecting A to B, with whatever seems best to roll on them for the time and place they're laid in. We may think we have come a long way since the first enthusiasts read Victorian industry journals, but we all still love the same thing. We've always loved our railways and always will. The twenty-first century has a long way to go yet.

The start of the twenty-first century marked the reopening of many lines as cycle routes and footpaths, but are the tables turning? Lines such as that pictured near Radstock, Somerset, are earmarked for reopening as a railway, though whether heritage or commuter is a contentious subject. (Author)

Further Reading

Below is a list of publications, both online and print, that may provide the reader with further insight and information on specific areas of the hobby mentioned throughout this title. Many of the print titles can be purchased from heritage railway museums and shops (including their websites), with profits often going towards the upkeep of stations and locomotives.

Bourgeois, F., *The Trainspotter's Notebook* (Transworld Publishers Ltd, 2023)

Cole, A., *Class 50 Locomotives* (Amberley Publishing, 2017)

Coleby, I., A. Stanistreet & I. Tabrett, *Tales of the West Somerset Railway* (West Somerset Steam Railway Trust, 2019)

Dolzall, G., & M. Danneman, *Steel Rails Across America: The Drama of Railroading in Spectacular Photos* (Kalmbach Publishing/Tide-mark Press, 1989)

Haddock, J., *Walsall's Engine Shed: Railwaymen's Memories 1877–1968* (The History Press, 2007)

Hayes, D., *The Pennines, Trains in the Landscape* (Amberley Publishing, 2022)

Jackson, A., *One Man's Railway: O Gauge in the Garden* (Amberley Publishing, 2021)

Jackson, A., *Signalling and Signal Boxes along the GER Routes* (Amberley Publishing, 2017)

Joy, David, *Settle-Carlisle in Colour* (The Dalesman Publishing Company Ltd, 1983)

Logan, I., & J. Glancey, *LOGOMOTIVE: Railroad Graphics and the American Dream* (Sheldrake Press, 2020)

Morris, R., *Miniature Railway Locomotives and Rolling Stock* (Amberley Publishing, 2018)

Pecorama, *First 40 years of the Beer Heights Light Railway* (PECO Publications & Publicity Ltd, 2015)

Thomas, R., *Memories from The End of the Line: Transforming a Picture into a Story* (Richard Thomas, 2021)

Your Guide to Railway Modelling and Layout Construction (PECO Publications & Publicity Ltd)

Various (including the author), *We Are Railfans* (2020) – wearerailfans.com

White, R. M., *The Roostery* (2023) – the-roostery.com

Acknowledgements

The author and publisher would like to thank the following people/organisations for permission to use copyright material in this book: Angus Duncan, Alan Land, Richard Szwejkowski, Dovetail Games and Absolute Aspects.

Every attempt has been made to seek permission for copyright material used in this book. However, if we have inadvertently used copyright material without permission/ acknowledgement, we apologise and we will make the necessary correction at the first opportunity.

Screenshots have been provided with the permission of Dovetail Games, a trading name of RailSimulator.com Ltd. All rights reserved.

A number of public domain works and works used under Creative Commons licence have been obtained by Pixabay and Wikimedia Commons using licenses valid at the time of writing.

The author would also like to thank the countless hobbyists and enthusiasts that they have encountered both personally and professionally over the period of a decade working from within the railway hobby. Their insights, knowledge and opinions on their passions, the enjoyment they get from them and the challenges they face from both within and beyond have been pivotal in the author's decision to create this work. Added to this are many personal experiences from the author himself. The author would encourage others to continue any of the conversations and topics raised here in works of their own.